Animal World

D1299622

Camels

Donna Bailey

STECK-VAUGHN
LIBRARY
A Division of Steck-Vaughn Company

A camel is often called a ship of the desert.
Like a ship, a camel carries goods and people.
Camels can go for a long time without
food or water.

There are two kinds of camels.
Camels that live in Africa have
one hump and are sometimes called
dromedaries.

The two-humped or Bactrian camel
lives in Asia.
A Bactrian camel is dark brown and has
shorter legs than the African camel.

In winter, Bactrian camels grow a
long, thick coat.
The coat protects the camel during
the bitterly cold winters of
the Gobi Desert.

African camels have thick, hairy skin that helps them live in the desert. Their skin keeps them from losing water by sweating. Their thick fur keeps them cool during the day and warm at night.

A camel's hump is filled with fat.
The camel changes this fat into food.
It stores water in the cells of its body.
The stored fat and water help a camel
travel several days without drinking
and even longer without eating.

At the end of a long journey,
the camel's hump may flop over because
it is no longer full of water and fat.

A camel can drink more than
30 gallons at one time.
The hump quickly fills with water and
becomes firm again.

Camels have two spreading, padded toes
on each foot.
These toes help them walk over
the loose sand in the desert.

A camel can see well and has
a good sense of smell.
Its bushy eyebrows and heavy lashes
protect its eyes.
A camel can close its nostrils into
tight slits during a sandstorm.

A camel's lips are covered with
thick, coarse hairs.
These protect the camel when it eats
the thorny scrub that grows in the sand.

Camels feed on shrubs and dry grass
that other animals would not eat.
They swallow their food quickly and
bring it up later to chew the cud.
When a camel is angry, it spits food
that it brings up from its stomach.

Camels can travel 70 miles a day.
They can carry over 400 pounds,
but with a heavy load they only travel
at about three miles an hour.

When it walks, a camel ambles.
It lifts its left legs off the ground
and then its right legs.
A camel can run as fast as 10 miles an hour.

There are still a few wild Bactrian camels.
They roam free in the Gobi Desert
and the highlands of central Asia.
The people who live there catch the camels
and use them to carry goods.

16

Thousands of years ago, people
used camels to carry goods.
Today camels are still important to
nomadic peoples like the Tuareg.
For hundreds of years, the Tuareg have
guided travelers across the Sahara Desert.

Many of the Tuareg people of North Africa
have now settled on farms.
But some Tuareg are still nomads.
They lead caravans of camels between
the desert cities of the Sahara.

18

Bedouin people have lived in Saudi Arabia and North Africa for hundreds of years. They used to travel with their herds of animals from one desert well to another. Most Bedouin now live in towns, but a few still keep camels and live in the desert.

The Bedouin take good care of their camels.

Water is scarce in the desert.

The Bedouin draw water from wells

to give their camels.

When the Bedouin were nomads, their camels gave them milk, meat, wool, leather, and dried manure for fuel.

Bedouin women wove camel hair into cloth.

Today most people in Saudi Arabia
do not use camels to carry
goods across the desert.
They use cars and trucks instead.

Some wealthy people in Saudi Arabia
still keep camels.
They hold camel races to see
which camel is fastest.

Nomads who live in Niger, in West Africa,
still cross the deserts in caravans.
Camels carry all the goods the people need.

24

The camels in this caravan in Niger
are carrying a load of beds.
The people are taking the beds to sell
in the market of the next town.

When the people of the Gabbra tribe in Kenya move, they load their homes onto camels. The camels carry all the tents and household goods.

The Gabbra stop at wells to fill up
their water containers.
The water must last until they reach
the next well.

Some people use camels to help draw water.
This camel is turning a wheel
which pumps water for the crops
onto the fields.

This farmer in Tunisia is using
his camel to pull a plow.

The people in northwest India and
Pakistan also have camels.
This camel in Pakistan is carrying
a heavy load of produce to market.

Many years ago, camels were taken to
Australia and some escaped into
the Australian Outback.
These camels live in the wild and
eat desert scrub.

In Australia, tourists can visit
camel farms and go on camel rides.
The people in Alice Springs hold
camel races like those in Saudi Arabia.

Index

Editorial Consultant: Donna Bailey
Executive Editor: Elizabeth Strauss
Project Editor: Becky Ward

Picture research by Jennifer Garratt
Designed by Richard Garratt Design

Photographs
Cover: OSF Picture Library (Eyal Bartov)
Bruce Coleman: title page, 6, 11 (Hans Reinhard); 12 (Eric Chrichton); 13 (John Newby); 17 (Prato 5092); 28 (J.L.G. Grande); 29 (Charles Henneghein); 30 (Bruce Coleman Ltd); 32 (Fritz Prenzell)
Hutchison Library: 2, 24 (Dave Brinicombe); 4, 5 (Brian Moser); 16, 18, 19, 20, 21, 25
OSF Picture Library: 7 (Steve Littewood); 8 (Anthony Bannister); 9 (Mike Brown)
Planet Earth: 3 (John Lythgoe); 23 (Hans Christian Heap); 31 (Transglobe/Deighmann)
Seaphot Limited: 10, 15 (Hans Christian Heap); 14 (G. Cafiero); 22 (Rod Salm); 26, 27 (Sean Avery)

Library of Congress Cataloging-in-Publication Data: Bailey, Donna. Camels / Donna Bailey. p. cm.—
(Animal world) Includes index. SUMMARY: Describes the two kinds of camels and how they have adapted to the rigors of desert life, while serving as mainstays in the lives of nomadic peoples. ISBN 0-8114-2644-0
1. Camels—Juvenile literature. [1. Camels.] I. Title. II. Series: Animal world (Austin, Tex.) SF401.C2B35
1991 636.2'95—dc20 90-22109 CIP AC

ISBN 0-8114-2644-0
Copyright 1991 Steck-Vaughn Company
Original copyright Heinemann Children's Reference 1991

1 2 3 4 5 6 7 8 9 0 LB 96 95 94 93 92 91